Ollie's Biblical Adventure Through Faith

Written by
P.A. Nadesan

Illustrated by
Jason Velazquez

Ollie's Biblical Adventure Through Faith
© 2022 by P.A. Nadesan

All rights reserved solely by the author. The author guarantees all contents are original and do not infringe upon the legal rights of any other person or work. No part of this book may be reproduced
in any form without the permission of the author. The views expressed in this book are not necessarily those of the publisher.

Printed in the United States of America.
ISBN-13: 978-0-5782938-5-1
Library of Congress Number: 2022907319

TMP Publishing
Melbourne, Florida

Hi, I am Oliver, but you can call me Ollie. I'm 7 years old and I love learning new things about God, don't you? Why don't we learn together?

I found out today that my mommy has a baby in her belly! She called it a funny word. She said she's pregnant. I expected mommy to be happy, but I noticed that she was really sad. I was wondering if it's because of the pregnancy.

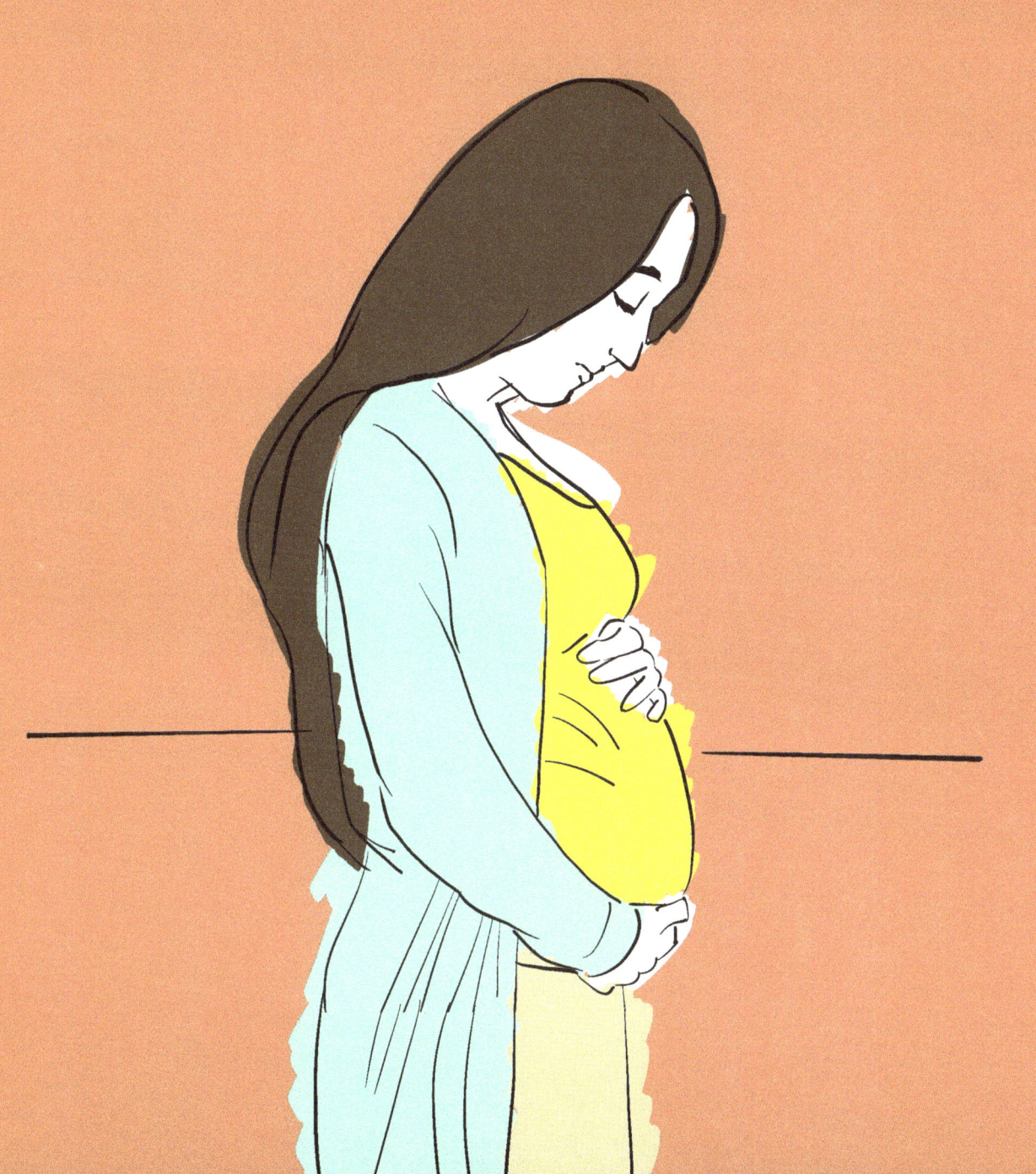

I went to ask daddy because I wanted to learn what was wrong. But he said we should all go to bed and pray because it was almost bedtime. He said they would talk to me tomorrow. So, when I prayed I also asked God to make mommy happy again.

Before going to sleep, this is how I pray. Say it with me! Now I lay me down to sleep, I pray the Lord my soul to keep, may angels guide me through the night and wake me with the morning light.

As everyone sleeps, Ollie begins to dream. He sees a lot of clouds and the sky is so beautifully blue! Suddenly, he hears someone speaking to him. It's coming from the man with the big white wings.

"Who are you?" Ollie asks.
"I am an angel; I am here to help you make your mommy happy again. First, I have to show you something."

Ollie grabs the angel by the hand, and he feels a lot of warmth and joy. The angel takes Ollie and walks him to a fluffy cloud. It looks like a marshmallow!

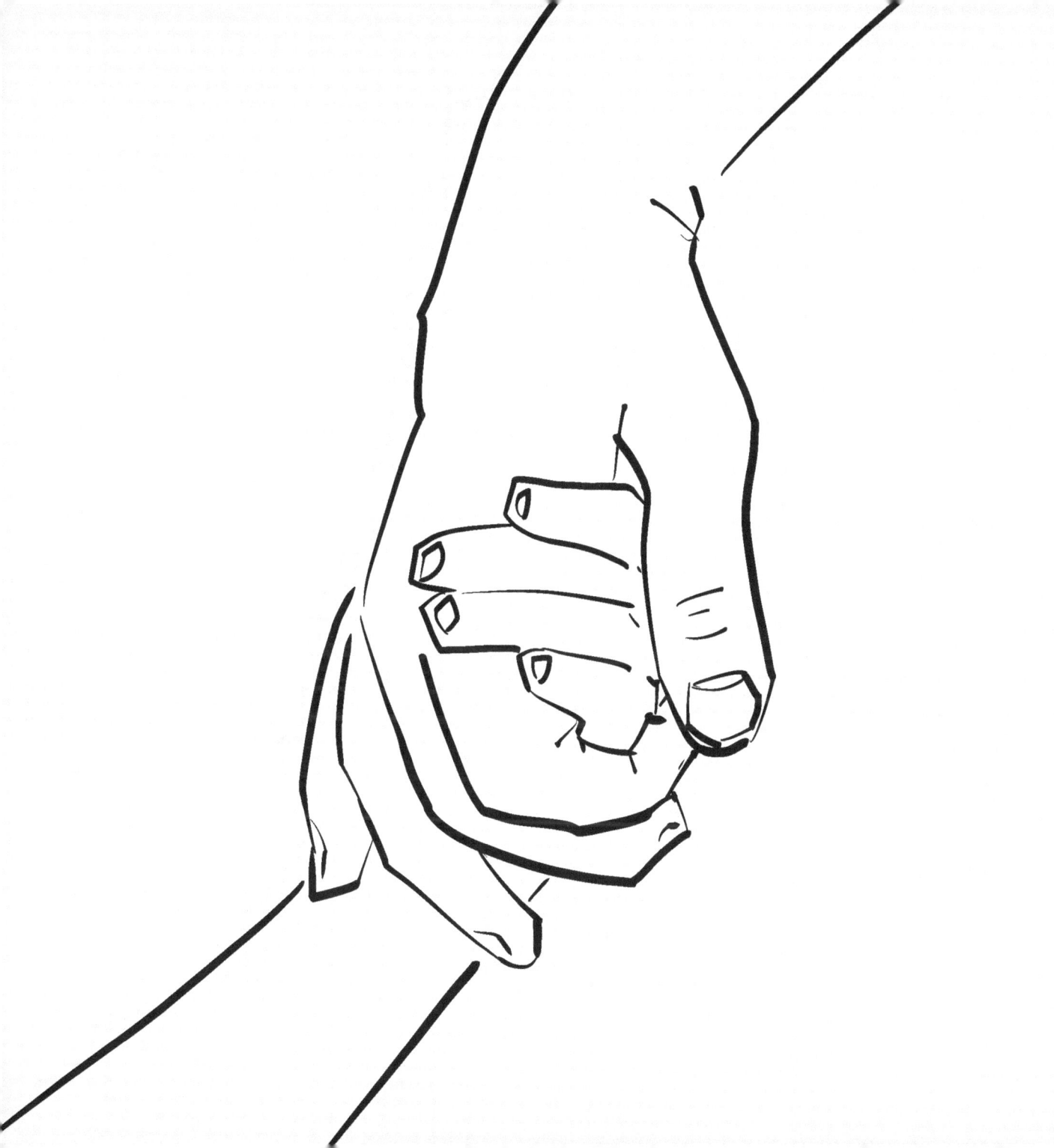

"Before I can tell you why your mommy is sad, I have to show you the story of a woman from many years ago," the angel said.

"This is Laura. Laura is a mom to three children."

Ollie says: "wow she's so pretty!"

The angel laughs and says: "yes, yes she is! But Laura, just like your mommy, has a baby in her belly."

"Oh!" Ollie exclaims. "That means she's pregnant!"

"yes very good. you're such a fast learner," the angel says. "So, you see Laura is carrying her fourth baby, but Laura is sick. This is causing her to lose hair and strength."

"well why doesn't God take her sickness away?" Ollie asked.

"well, if God does that she will not learn the lesson that he's trying to teach her."

"well, what lesson is that angel?"

The angel replied: "the lesson of faith."

"what's faith?" asked Ollie.

"Well according to God's word, faith is the substance of things hoped for, it is the evidence of things not seen. This means that even though you can't see God or touch him like you can with your family, you can still trust him to help you through everything."

Ollie looks at the angel very confused.

"Why don't I show you?" the angel chuckles.

"When Laura was about four months pregnant she got really scared because the baby was not moving. Laura and her aunt prayed very hard. After seven minutes the baby girl began to move again. Laura knew that God would always protect those who are very faithful to him. However, God had one more test."

"Let's look here when Laura is with her doctor. He's asking her not to keep the baby and to save herself. A lot of people in the family have said the same thing. Laura is sad because she feels like she has to try to choose the best thing to do."

"Laura decided that no matter what happens, she's going to keep the baby because God has blessed her with this baby. See here, now she's asking everyone she knows to please pray for her."

"Every day Laura asked God to keep her baby alive, even if that meant she might never get to meet this baby. She decided that she had lived long enough, and she wanted to give her baby girl a chance at life. God heard all of the prayers, but he especially heard Laura's prayers. Her faith was so strong that God decided to bless her with the strength to keep the baby healthy."

"When Laura's baby girl was born, Laura was still very sick. Even after the baby was one year old, Laura was fighting her sickness. Laura prayed to God again with all her strength and all her faith."

"This time she asked God to help her live until her baby girl was at least 13 years old so that she could guide her until she was old enough to know right from wrong. Just old enough that she could understand how to take care of herself. Again, God heard her and blessed her, but this time he blessed her to not be sick anymore. He blessed her so much because of her faith in him, that he allowed her to live and see her grandchildren."

"Wow!" Ollie said. "So, she had a lot of faith and knew that God would take care of everything and because of that God blessed her?"

"Yes!" said the angel.

"Wait! But what was her baby girl's name? You never told me."

"Well Ollie, I'm glad you asked. Her baby girl grew up and this is what she looks like now."

"Hey, that's my mommy!" Ollie yelled. "So, does that mean that the story is about my Grandma Laura?"

"Yes Ollie, that is your grandma Laura. Her baby girl is your mommy, and you are Laura's grandson. Your mom is not sad that she's pregnant, she's sad because the doctor said that the baby most likely will not make it."

"But mommy just has to follow Grandma Laura's story and have faith that God will help her!" Oliver exclaimed.

"That is correct, and your mommy has been praying but she is still really sad. To make your mommy happy again just tell her what God's word has taught you."

The next morning Ollie woke up and ran to his parents room, he jumped with excitement and said: "Mommy I know why you're sad." "My friend Angel said to always remember God's word which says that faith is the substance of things hoped for and the evidence of things not seen."

"My baby brother is going to be okay; we just have to have faith in God!"

Ollie's mommy and daddy hugged him and cried tears of joy because they knew that God had heard their prayers, and everything would be okay.

A little help from the Angel

Did you know that this story is based on the word of God? That's right! If you have a Bible or if mom and dad have a Bible, you can go to the book of Hebrews and look up chapter eleven and verse one (Hebrews 11:1). It says:

"Now faith is the substance of things hoped for, the evidence of things not seen."

So, in other words, faith is when we trust God with all of our heart even though we can't see Him.

There were other words that we used to show this beautiful story that you might not be familiar with, such as:

Pregnant – which is when a mommy has a baby in her stomach

Pregnancy – is the time that goes by with mommy carrying the baby in her tummy until the baby is born

www.ingramcontent.com/pod-product-compliance
Lightning Source LLC
Chambersburg PA
CBHW061808290426
44109CB00031B/2968